A CRUISE ALONG THE
MANCHESTER SHIP CANAL

By

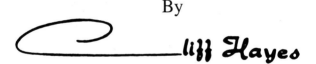
Cliff Hayes

MERSEY FERRIES

Published by Mersey Ferrries Ltd.,
Victoria Place
Seacombe Wallasey
L44 6QY
Tel: 0151 630 1030

ISDN 0952 6573 17

written by Cliff Hayes

photographs and maps suplied by

book prepared by

0161 862 9399

Printed by
Ashford Colour Press Ltd
Unit 600, Fareham Reach,
Gosport,
Hants. PO13 0FW.
Tel: 01329 229700 Fax: 01329 229777

Mersey Ferries is an operating subsidiary of Merseyside Passenger Service Transport Executive
Registered Office 24 Hamilton Garden, Liverpool L3 2AN.

CONTENTS

ON BEHALF OF THE MANCHESTER SHIP CANAL . . . . Page 3

WELCOME ABOARD . . . . Page 5

INTRODUCTION . . . . Page 6

MAPS OF THE FULL SHIP CANAL . . . . Page 9

THE MERSEY FERRIES . . . . Page 12

THE MANCHESTER SHIP CANAL . . . . Page 17

YOUR JOURNEY TODAY . . . . Page 20

MANCHESTER DOCKS . . . . Page 41

PICTURES FROM THE PAST . . . . Page 49

UNUSUAL VISITORS . . . . Page 53

Foreword

I am delighted to contribute a foreword to this guide book and commentary. As a boy who grew up near the Canal within the sound of ships' sirens, I have always been aware of its romance and the compelling story of how, against all odds, it triumphantly came into being, and now, as Chairman of the Company, I am immensely proud of the heritage of which I and my colleagues are custodians.

It is no exaggeration to describe the Canal as liquid history, a 36 mile long narrative, stirring in its tale, of how our Victorian forefathers made Manchester into Britain's third largest port. The tale of the 16,000 men who laboured for seven long years on the ''Big Ditch'' so that the oceans' mightiest ships could sail to the very heart of our region and of the prosperity which came in its wake.

A stirring tale indeed! Enjoy your trip!

Robert Hough
Chairman of the Manchester Ship Canal Company

WELCOME ABOARD

'HEAVE TO ME HEARTIES'

WELCOME aboard your Mersey ferry, and the start of your cruise.

We at Mersey Ferries are a friendly lot and have made sure that everything possible has been put into place to make your day a memorable one. We have even had a word with the weather man, but don't blame us if he gets it wrong.

From the Captain of the ship right through to every member of the crew, all are dedicated to making your cruise an enjoyable experience. We have on board a Ship Canal Pilot, trained to make sure that we have a smooth and safe passage. We also have a Mersey Guide to provide a commentary that will inform, amuse and entertain you, and help you get much more out of the day. The Manchester Ship Canal Company have Lock Masters and staff at each of the five locks that we pass through to ensure a smooth passage.

The catering staff are also friendly and attentive, just waiting to serve you. Please do not ask about 'Duty Free' drink, that only happens when we turn the wrong way from the landing stage and head over the 'Bar' (The Mersey Bar) not the Public Bar!

The engineers, the deck hands, all the Mersey Ferries family hope you enjoy your Cruise with us and wish you . . . . . .

Bon Voyage!

INTRODUCTION

THIS booklet is designed for those of you who are sailing the Manchester Ship Canal with Mersey Ferries along what is one of the wonderful feats of engineering and sheer hard work that came out of the late Victorian period. It has been written for you to get even more enjoyment out of the day by knowing the route of your journey and what is around you as you traverse the 35 miles between Liverpool and Manchester or Manchester to Liverpool.

It will also serve as a reminder of your interesting day out, and bring back happy memories of a unique experience. The Manchester Ship Canal is like a maritime motorway of a century ago. Our forefathers took the rivers Irwell and Mersey, and deepened, straightened and cut them to run where it was convenient for man and the ships that served the needs of a growing nation.

It will also, we hope be an enjoyable read for anyone interested in the history of the Ship Canal, and the rise and fall of the Manchester Docks. If you are not travelling the Canal and just reading the book then maybe this will give you an insight into how much there is to see and learn on your 'cruise' along the Manchester Ship Canal and retrace those, albeit watery, footsteps laid down over a century before by men of great vision, who saw that the world needed the goods and services that Manchester and Lancashire were producing and wanted to get them out to the four corners of the globe as quickly as possible.

The maps section, starting on page 23 takes you from Liverpool up to Salford docks. It does work the other way, a lot of trouble has been taken so that each double page is complete in itself and can be read backwards from page 45 for anyone taking the journey from Manchester down the Canal to Liverpool.

Manchester Ship Canal Docking facilities were referred to by the company as Manchester Docks, but in reality they were 97% inside the Salford border. The company always called them Manchester Docks, but to the workers and people around them they were Salford Docks. Please keep this in mind as we talk about the upper end of the Ship Canal.

WHERE DID IT ALL START?

TO UNDERSTAND the history of Mersey Ferries, you need to look at a map of the Mersey and its banks in the 1600s. As you can see on the map overleaf both the Bidston and Birkenhead Pools were quite wide and needed to be crossed. The land between these two waters was used as a crossing point even before the Monk's ferry.

The Priory at Birkenhead was founded in around 1150 by Royal License and although they received the rights to erect a lodging house for travellers in 1313, it was not until 1330 that they received the ferry rights, for which they had to pay the Crown. Before 1330 Robert de Ferrers had held the concession but lost it in 1266 to Edmund, Earl of Lancashire. Thomas son of Edmund rebelled against the King and had the ferry rights taken off him in 1323. This led to the splitting of the rights, the monks charter being challenged by William Lascelles, and although his objection was turned down, the rights to the ferry from the north bank of the Wallasey pool were sold separately to the Earl of Chester and the king was pleased that he had raised money twice.

'The Seccom Ferry' originally crossed over to Birkenhead from where you took the Monks Ferry to Liverpool. The fact that the two ferries were now separate and run by different concerns led, in the long-term, to the two corporations of Wallasey & Birkenhead running side by side. When the rights to the ferry were passed on, and they went through many hands, they were always regarded as separate, with the dividing line being where it was placed in 1330, right down the middle of the pool at Tokesford (Wallasey Pool).

The Stanleys of Hooton, the Vyners of Bidston and even Ralph Worsley of Worsley, Manchester, ran the ferries over the next 400 years. At the time of the Reformation in 1536 the income from ferry passengers was estimated to be over £5 per year. The Liverpool rights to a ferry were sold at auction on May 17th, 1544, but sold again to the Molyneux family c.1590.

In 1626 there was unrest and this led to a public meeting where the Liverpool boatmen demanded an end to undercutting and that the 'Home' boat always got the job first. Rivalry and feuding went on until the 1800s.

The ferry to Birkenhead finally passed to the Corporation who ran it for many years. Completely separate were the Wallasey Ferries whose landing stages included Seacombe, Egremont and New Brighton. It is the two Corporations, Wallasey and Birkenhead, who ran the service, including the goods and cargo boats which carried so much of the traffic before the opening of the Mersey Tunnel in 1934. On 1st December 1968, the two ferry services were merged under the Merseytravel Transport Authority, and Mersey Ferries was born.

Liverpool Pier Head in the Swinging Sixties.

A crowded M.V. 'Egremont' on a trip along the Ship Canal in 1965.

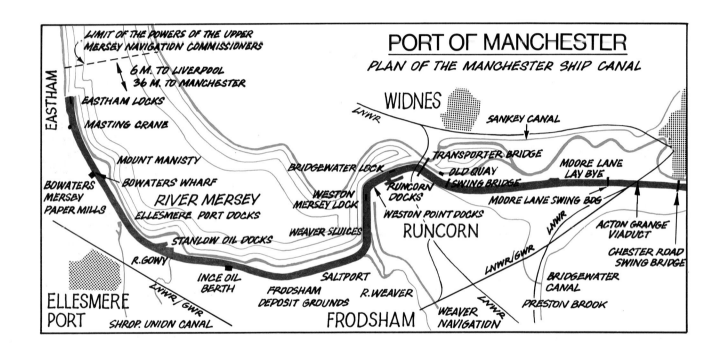

PORT OF MANCHESTER

PLAN OF THE MANCHESTER SHIP CANAL

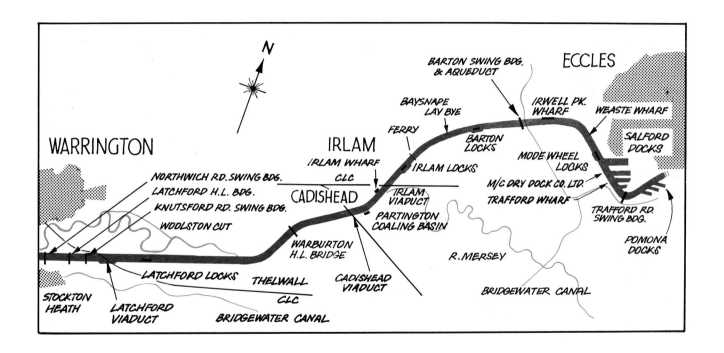

FACTS AND FIGURES OF THE CANAL'S CONSTRUCTION

6,300 wagons were employed
16,000 plus, men and boys worked on the construction
180 steam locomotives were involved
5,000 wheelbarrows worked, shifting earth.
230 miles of temporary track laid
200 horses were kept and stabled
36 miles of elongated dock
320 portable lights (2,000 candle-power) for night work.

The PLANT included:
    4 floating dredgers
    7 land dredgers
  96 steam driven excavators
192 portable power engines.
212 steam pumps to deal with the water.
  59 pile-driving engines.
        Total value over £1,300,000.

To keep the steam engines and drivers, etc going the canal construction needed 10,000 tons of coal PER MONTH.

A 'Brick Farm' was started at Thelwall and produced 70,000,000 bricks used in the construction of the canal and bridges that spanned it.

220,000 cubic yards of stone-work and masonry were used and 1,250,000 cubic yards of concrete were mixed and used.

16,000 labourers worked on the canal at the height of construction. Average wage for the navvies was four and a half-pence per hour for a 10 hour day. Besides pneumonia and rheumatics that affected the men, 3,000 major accidents were treated in the Base Hospital. More than 130 men died through accidents during construction.

10 miles of embankment keep the River Mersey back on the Runcorn bend,13,000 piles had to be driven into the river bed to hold the embankment in place.
The section beneath the railway bridge here is the narrowest part of the canal.

An estimated 51,603,747 cubic yards of earth, sandstone rock and other materials were excavated, with a weight of approximately 77,000,000 tons.

Along the canal today there are 6 swing bridges, 1 swing aqueduct and 1 lifting bridge (Centenary Bridge), 2 high level cantilever road bridges, 2 motorway viaducts, 1 high level road bridge and 5 railway bridges.

There are five locks including Eastham, the entrance lock.
They lift (or drop) ships 60ft from Salford Dock to Eastham Locks.

1710 First mention of the possibillity of a Ship Canal from Manchester to the sea.
1734 Ships of upto 50 tons were able to sail into Manchester via the Mersey and Irwell Navigation.
1766 A passenger carrying service began on the Bridgewater Canal from Manchester.
1840 The first scheme for a Ship Canal from Manchester was presented by a Mr Palmer and Mr Batemen.
1879 Manchester businessmen voted to support the plans for a Ship Canal.
1882 (June 27th) Daniel Adamson called his famous meeting to form a provisional Ship Canal Committee.
1885 (August 6th) The Ship Canal Bill finally received Royal assent.
1887 (November 11th) Work finally began on the construction of the Manchester Ship Canal.
1893 (November 11th) The last dry cutting was made in the building of the Ship Canal.
1893 (November 25th) The Canal was filled end-to-end with water.
1893 (December 7th) Ship Canal directors made the first ever trip from end-to-end of the Canal (on a Mersey ferry of course).
1894 (January 1st) The Manchester Ship Canal opened to traffic with a great display of ships. Thousands of people turned out to watch.
1894 (May 1st) Queen Victoria visited Salford Docks and declared the Ship Canal officially open.

YOUR FLOATING CONVEYANCE

YOUR transport on this journey through time will be one of the well maintained vessels from the Mersey Ferries fleet. To introduce you to your maritime conveyance, your ship, may we present the ships that week in week out provide such a needed and stirling service across the River Mersey between Liverpool, Wallasey and Birkenhead. This is a day out for the ship as well as its passengers, and just between you and me, I think they enjoy the day as much as you do.

M.V. MOUNTWOOD. Named after an area near Bebbington on the Wirral.
Built at Dartmouth, and launched on to the River Dart on July 6th, 1959, she is the oldest of the sisters but only by three months. She arrived in the River Mersey to begin her work in 1960 and has been re-fitted and modernised over the years. Length: 152ft long, beam 40ft. Gross tonnage: 464. Three decks and can carry 750 passengers.

M.V. WOODCHURCH. Again named after an area on the Wirral, just to the south of Birkenhead. She was launched into the River Dart on October 29th, 1959 and after fitting out followed her sister to the River Mersey in 1960.
Length: 152ft long, beam 40ft.
Gross tonnage: 464. Three decks and can safely and comfortably carry 750 passengers.
Both these two ships have two eight cylinder diesel engines, built by Crossley Bros. of Manchester. These drive the twin screws at almost 1,400 B.H.P. (horse power).

M.V. OVERCHURCH. A Wirral lady in every way, named after an area, south of Bidston Hill, near Morton. Built locally at Cammell Laird's shipyard in Birkenhead she joined the fleet in 1962.

The 'Overchurch' is slightly longer and heavier than the other two and is very well suited to the canal cruise.

All three work at an average of 12 knots as they cross the Mersey on their daily tasks. They travel the Ship Canal at about ten knots, a speed calculated to do the least damage with the ship's wash on the canal banks.

THE MANCHESTER SHIP CANAL

Manchester like Liverpool is set on the banks of a river, but whereas the River Mersey, that faces the city of Liverpool, is broad, tidal, and only a few miles from the open sea, the River Irwell that flows between Manchester and Salford is a slow, winding and sluggish river that meanders down to the sea. Man by his very nature has always been drawn to travelling and moving on water, and what is easier than going with the flow of a river and out to the big wide ocean. Not so easy when that river has great sweeping curves with sand banks and shallows that can be crossed by foot.

As early as 1650 there were plans to deepen the rivers of the North. Coastal trading was on the increase, and as roads were poor and slow, transport by boat was a popular alternative. Passengers as well as cargoes could be transported for miles in-land from the sea ports along rivers that could be made navigable.

In 1712, Thomas Steers, the man who built Liverpool's first dock made a survey of the rivers Douglas, Weaver and Mersey to plan how to use these rivers for the advancement of trade in the North West. In 1721 an Act of Parliament was passed to make the rivers Mersey and Irwell more navigable to boats up 500 tons.

A River Act was not the same as a Canal Act, because it had to preserve the rights of mill owners who took water from the rivers to power their mills. Cutting off a long slow bend in a river could mean depriving a mill of water throwing hundreds of people out of work. The canalisation and deepening of the rivers Mersey and Irwell would have to be handled very carefully because of these considerations.

In 1724 work began on constructing 8 locks 13ft x 85ft, and some 'cuts' to enable ships to sail right into Manchester, and a receiving quay was built, at the bottom of what we now know as Quay Street. The money for this venture was put forward by the merchants of Manchester who were always looking for cheaper methods of transportation of their goods. There was much trial and error at this time. The cutting out of the longer slower bends sometimes brought about much flooding of low lying areas, which happened more than once. The River Mersey was tidal until just above Warrington and the system of straightening and deepening the river worked, but the Warrington to Manchester stretch often ran out of water in the summer and boats were stranded for days at a time. The Mersey & Irwell Navigation Company constructed 8 weirs alongside its locks to try and keep the water in each section. Even these measures did not always work, and barges were often seen dumping some of their cargoes to get them through the shallows. This dumping of coal, and other cargoes, over-board created even more problems to the waterway.

By 1779 there were two waterways between Manchester and Runcorn,

1) The Bridgewater Canal with no locks from Castlefield, Manchester through to Lymm and south to Warrington and Runcorn. There you had to go down 8 locks

to join up with the River Mersey. Bridgewater House, which was for so long the offices of the Manchester Ship Canal Company was built where the canal joined the River Mersey at Runcorn.

2) The rival route was the Mersey & Irwell Navigation which ran from Quay Street, Manchester to Runcorn where the smaller ships transferred their cargoes to larger steam ships for transportation to Liverpool and beyond.

Both routes offered a journey time to Liverpool of one day, as travelling in daylight hours was something of a necessity at this time.

One land-mark incident was the delivery in 1841 of a consignment of potatoes direct from Dublin to Manchester in a 500 ton ship. Coal from Pendleton Pit was loaded at Quay Street for the return journey to Ireland.

With the opening of the railways and the construction of lines to most of Lancashire, it should have been that the need for any other means of transport became obsolete. The inland canals constructed after the Bridgewater Canal at the end of the 1700's were doing their work well. Industrial loads were being kept off the poor roads, large bulk deliveries were being made at low costs and it was proving a reasonably safe mode of transport. These canals brought about a thriving prosperity in the few years (1790-1830) that they ruled and dominated the movement of imports and exports. Railways should have been the answer to Manchester's problem of getting in the raw cotton, and getting out the finished cotton goods to the world. The fact that they were not

was due to the very high charges levied at Liverpool and the surcharges put on by the railway.

There was more than one contributing factor to the economic depression which settled over Manchester around 1865, but it must be said that the rail charges and port charges at Liverpool were a major factor.

The fact that Oldham spinners could send a buyer to Bremen and Le Havre and ship cotton through Hull and

Daniel Adamson father of the Ship Canal

across the Pennines and save 7d on each 28lb sack was testiment to the high charges at Liverpool. Cotton goods were costing Manchester merchants more to move from their mill to the ship at Liverpool than from Liverpool to Calcutta or Sydney, Australia.

Inland Lancashire and Manchester in particular started to

die as far as trade was concerned. Factories closed down, and moved to Liverpool, Preston and the coast. People put out of work moved to where the new factories offered employment. In 1875 there were empty houses and dwellings all over central Manchester. Factories stood empty and the old 'navigation' was in poor condition, with the river silting up and wanting money desperately spending on dredging. Money that no one seemed willing to put up.

After one or two half-hearted attempts a champion emerged, who had the leadership and imagination to pull Manchester out of this depression. On June 27, 1882 Daniel Adamson presided over a meeting at his home 'The Towers', Didsbury, of about fifty people whom he thought could put together, and back, the plan for a ship canal from Manchester to the sea. The mayors of all the Lancashire towns concerned were there, plus engineers, industrialists and investors, all wisely chosen. Adamson himself addressed the meeting and spoke passionately on the need for a canal. Engineers pointed out the route and the problems involved, and after discussion a committee was set up to take the plans forward the Manchester Ship Canal was born!

The next step was to over-come the powerful land owners in their way, and to start lobbying against the wealthy and influential Liverpool merchants. It did not happen over night, and there were many set backs. If it had not have been for the tenacity and fortitued of certain men in that Victorian industrial atmosphere, the canal would never have been completed.

Marshall Stevens the man who talked the plans through Parliment

19

THE MANCHESTER SHIP CANAL COMPANY

On a cold day in November 1887 a party of men gathered at a spot near to Eastham on the Wirral. Watched by workmen, recently taken on and waiting to begin work, and by a few invited guests, Lord Egerton of Tatton, who had by then taken over as chairman of the Ship Canal Company, ceremoniously cut the first sod of the new water-way. Tradition has it that a navvy was brought forward after he had pushed the spade in, and finished off the cutting by lifting the sod. The soil was put into a new wheel barrow and Leader Williams, the engineer, wheeled it away. Work had at last started on the Ship Canal, over five years after Daniel Adamson had called a meeting at his home in Didsbury to make initial plans for the water-way, and two years after an Act of Parliament was passed enabling land to be purchased along its route.

The construction of the canal was divided into nine sections (later reduced to eight) and Thomas Andrew Walker, the contractor appointed for the job had estimated that it would take four and a half years to complete the 36 mile project.

Walker had been the contractor on the Severn Tunnel and Metropolitan Underground in London and other similar projects and was a liked and well respected man. He had been assembling equipment for some months and work started immediately at four different points, Warrington, Warburton and Salford as well as at Eastham. Walker quickly constructed railway lines joining these sites which were vital to shift men and gear as well as remove the vast amounts of soil from the diggings. Most of the men toiled with picks and shovels, but Walker was always foremost in the introduction of mechanical aids whenever possible to help in the gigantic task. The story of the of the building of the Manchester Ship Canal is well told in other books such as "100 Years of the Manchester Ship Canal" by Ted Gray.

Thomas Walker knew his workforce and cared for them, which was more than most other contractors at the time did. He built decent huts for the men to live in. A wooden chapel was built at each camp, and he made sure that his men had the time to attend. He was the first to erect First Aid Posts at each work site, with a first aider on hand to attend any accidents, and a doctor attended once or twice a week. Any navvy who was injured and could no longer cope with the heavy work was found another lighter job, and it is even recorded that Walker, on more than one occasion sent money to the widows of men killed during construction. Injured men became known as "Walker's Fragments" or "Walker's Wounded" and were a sign to the men that even if they were injured they would not be thrown out without hope of earning a wage. All these things assured Walker of a willing and hard-working workforce.

Walker engaged a Liverpool surgeon, Robert Jones to run and organise three site hospitals that he had erected along the railway lines. Jones later became famous for his work with bone fractures and splints in WW1 which saved thousands of lives.

The construction of the Ship Canal was no easy task and was fraught with many problems. Opposing land owners still put obstructions in the Canal's way. There were accidents with water flooding into sections before they were ready. Dams bursting between the River Mersey and the canal and many railway accidents. But slowly and surely the sections came together. The Ellesmere Port section was the first flooded on 19th June 1891 and Eastham Locks were flooded a month later. The first ship through them to berth at Ellesmere Port was on July 16th that year. By September 1891 the canal had reached the mouth of the River Weaver, and here a whole 'shanty town' grew up. It became known at 'Saltport' because of the salt that was transported down the Weaver from the salt mines in Nantwich, Northwich and Middlewich. The town, of which today there is little trace, was a busy place, with a chapel, offices, bank as well as sleeping quarters.

Runcorn was still working as a port and channels had to be kept open for shipping until the Canal was ready to handle it. Extra locks were built into the outside canal wall to let ships from Runcorn Old Dock out into the River Mersey at high tide, saving them the journey up the canal to Eastham.

July 1893 saw Runcorn cut off by the Canal, November saw the Canal filled end to end and on December 7th, 1893, roughly six years after the first sod had been cut, the directors of the Ship Canal Company made a journey of its full length.

The Manchester Ship Canal opened on January 1st, 1894, and the directors on board Samuel Platt's yacht the 'Norseman', led a Parade of 71 ships from Latchford up to Salford. The second ship that day was a Mersey ferry the 'Snowdrop' carrying the mayors of Lancashire towns along with other distinguished officials. The co-operative movement even combined business with pleasure and unloaded a cargo of tea from the newly bought ship the 'Pioneer'.

Queen Victoria declared the Canal officially open on May 21st 1894, but by then it was settling down well and was even showing a profit. The Queen arrived at Victoria Station, drove through Salford, crossed the docks on the Royal Yacht 'Enchantress', and knighted the mayors of Salford and Manchester. She then retraced her steps back through Salford to London Road Station and back South. The whole thing took place in just a few hours. Many reports of the day claimed that the Queen arrived in her yacht but she actually only crossed the Docks in it.

The Manchester Ship Canal is one of the greatest of the Victorian engineering feats. Sailing on it is a pleasure and a privilege that we take too easy for granted. What we must also keep in mind is that the upper reaches are the River Irwell as well and the middle section is the River Mersey. While the canal was being constructed thousands of gallons of the river water had to be kept back, channelled away and controlled. Marvel ladies and gentlemen at one of the man-made wonders of this world of ours.

The gangway and welcoming view as you board the ferry.

YOUR JOURNEY TODAY

To travel the whole length of anything you have to start at one end and whether you start at the Liverpool or the Manchester end of the Manchester Ship Canal, you are undertaking a very unique journey. The Ship Canal is the longest, man made stretch of navigable river/canal in Britain, a very special piece of engineering. We must not forget that it is also the River Irwell, with its millions of gallons of water, pouring out from city centre Manchester, having to be managed, cosseted, preserved, controlled all the way to Ellesmere Port. This is not a gentle, easy relationship. Some days the river is in full flow and getting the fresh, fast flowing water, gathered from the hills of Rawtenstall and around Bury, down to the sea, is an exciting and exhilarating job. Opening sluices and lock gates to be just in front of flood waters keeps man and the latest computers on their toes. Some days the supply is sluggish, the rivers seem to hold on to their precious supply of life-giving liquid. Lock gates are shut and channels are blocked to keep the precious water in the Canal and keep the levels on the Canal sections at working heights.

There is not another canal in England where a river (the River Mersey) flows into it, and then later is allowed, by weirs, to flow out, and back along its original course. You will travel today, the Super Highway, constructed a hundred plus years ago, you will ride the Maritime Motorway that kept Manchester going in the lean years at the end of the Victorian period. All around you today is history and marvellous engineering feats. Sometime in your journey try closing your eyes and imagining what it was like for the directors of the Ship Canal who on December 7th 1893, made, in the Wallasey ferry 'Snowdrop', the very first journey from Liverpool to Manchester. The very same trip that you are making today aboard a modern ferry. The pride in their hearts that the project was complete at last after seven years of struggle. The relief that now their investment may start to pay back some of the thousands of £s they had each put into the dream.

Ship Canal Passenger Steamer Co. (1893) Ltd.
(The Manchester Company.)

ROYAL VISIT TO THE CANAL.

On the 21st MAY, the following Steamers will (weather and other circumstances permitting) sail from

LIVERPOOL (PRINCE'S LANDING STAGE) **for MANCHESTER**

At the hours named. On reaching the Docks they will be moored where the passengers can obtain a view of the proceedings in connection with the Queen's Visit :—

"FLYING FALCON"	... ...	leaving at 9
"BLACK PRINCE"	... ...	" 9-30
"EAGLE"	... ...	" 10

Inclusive Fare, on the "Flying Falcon" and "Black Prince," 5/-; on the "Eagle," 6/- each.

LIGHT REFRESHMENTS ON BOARD.

The following Steamers will take passengers on board at Nos. 1 and 3 Docks, Pomona, (Cornbrook entrance), at 3-15, viz. :—

"Daniel Adamson," "Fairy Queen," and "Manx Fairy."

These Steamers will also be well placed in the Docks so as to witness the ceremony.

Fare on the "**Daniel Adamson,**" 7/6; young people under 15, 4/-. On the "**Fairy Queen**" and "**Manx Fairy**," 5/- each. (No half fares.)

Tea and other Refreshments will be provided on board.

The attractive Band of the Training Ship "**Indefatigable**" will be on board the "**Daniel Adamson.**"

By special arrangement with the Ship Canal Company, this Company's Irwell River Steamers will also convey guests from **Bailey Bridge** (Nemesis Rowing Club Stage), to their respective Stands in the Docks from 1 till 4 p.m. **Fare 1/-.** These Tickets may now be obtained from Messrs. Forsyth Brothers, Deansgate, or at the Offices of the Company as under.

The Steamers "**Hotspur,**" "**Water Lily,**" and "**St. Mawes Castle,**" will also convey Ticket Holders from Nos. 1 and 2 Docks, Pomona, to the Grand Stands from 1 till 3 o'clock. **Fare 1/-.**

All the above Steamers will take up passengers at the Pomona Docks, between 7 and 8 p.m., and convey them to the Salford Docks to witness the Fireworks Display. **Fare 1/-.**

Tickets and full particulars may be obtained at the Offices of the Company, 46, Brown Street, or Trafford Wharf, or from the Company's Agents, SWAN & LEACH, LTD., Albert Square, and 216, Stretford Road, Manchester.

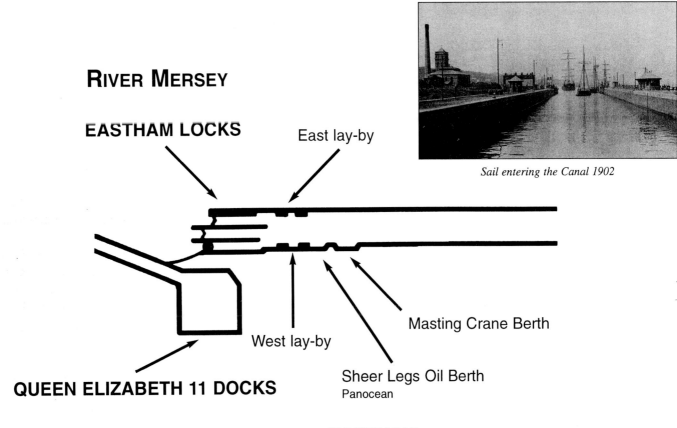

RIVER MERSEY

EASTHAM LOCKS

East lay-by

Sail entering the Canal 1902

Masting Crane Berth

West lay-by

QUEEN ELIZABETH 11 DOCKS

Sheer Legs Oil Berth
Panocean

EASTHAM

24

EASTHAM LOCKS: flooded for the first time on July 2nd, 1891, and the first ship went through to Ellesmere Port on July 16th, 1891. When these locks opened there were 3 locks or chambers as they were described then. The inner (150ft x 30ft) one which was for small barges, that had come down the Shropshire Canal, is no longer used.

The distance we rise in the locks depends of course on the height of the tide as we enter. When the Canal was very busy, ships in the Canal were allowed out on the rising tide, the smallest first and the largest in the minutes before high water. At the turn of the tide vessels waiting to enter the Canal started entering the locks, the largest first and so on. This, of course, made sense as it cleared the mouth of the Eastham lay-by and Canal making more room for incoming ships, and it made sure the least amount of water was released from the canal.

Though the Canal is 36 miles long it has always been controlled and run as if it were one large harbour. Movements internally (Runcorn to Ellesmere Port etc.,) are handled as crossing a harbour and every movement must be radioed to the same control centre which is the white building on the North side of the locks. Our ship will be in contact with this control centre throughout the whole journey. Once inside the Eastham Locks you are technically in Manchester Docks.

Crossing the River Mersey our captain has been controlling the vessel, but now we are in the Ship Canal we come under the control of our canal pilot. I know that we are not likely to get lost along the Ship Canal (just follow the wall on the north) but there are many important matters to deal with. These highly trained and dedicated pilots are masters of their craft of guiding the vessels safely to and from Eastham to their respective berths. They control our speed along the canal, as they know where the banks are in need of care and slow us down to make our wash smaller. They know how the river is flowing and what if any resistance or assistance our vessel will get, and at each lock it is the pilot who controls speed and direction, so that we slide smoothly into the locks at just the right amount of knots. The pilot will also know exactly where we can pass other vessels safely, and where the shallows are, and guide us expertly along our way. We are safe in the hands of the canal pilots, and it is a comforting thought.

On the South side of the locks you see the Queen Elizabeth II Dock. This dock, specially designed to handle liquid petroleum products, has its own independent entrance from the River Mersey and has four berths which can handle ships up to 900ft long. The tanks are hidden below ground and the berths are connected directly to various refiners situated along the canal side.

Just a short way along the Canal you have a tall crane on the South side. This is the de-masting crane and ships suspected of having funnels or masts over 70ft high would have them lifted off here and left on the Canal side until they were ready to leave and enter the Mersey. The crane can handle up to 30 tons, at 35ft reach and 15 tons at its maximum stretch of 64ft.

*An aerial view of the new dock at Ellesmere Port,
opened 26th May 1933 by Oliver Stanley, the
Minister of Transport at the time.*

RIVER MERSEY

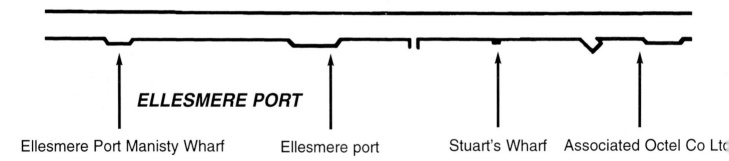

ELLESMERE PORT

Ellesmere Port Manisty Wharf   Ellesmere port   Stuart's Wharf   Associated Octel Co Ltd

The divide between the Canal and river just here is known as Pool Hall Embankment and then on the outside of the canal is a large hill known as Mount Manisty. The earth dug out to shape the Ship Canal was a problem for the engineers in charge of each section. Sometimes extra earth was needed for ballast so soil and rocks had to be moved from one part to another especially in the Ellesmere section. There were some rocks (Pool Hall Rocks) on the Mersey side of the Canal and it was decided to put (store) earth on them in case it was needed. This reserve grew and grew and ended up as a 'hill' on the Canal embankment. The men decided to call it 'Mount Manisty' in honour of Mr Edward Manisty, who was the contractor's agent for that section. It was his job to deal with all supplies and suppliers and get rid of all the earth and he did his job well and was scrupulously honest. He and his wife really took the men's welfare to heart and did a lot for them. They even organised entertainment at Eastham as an alternative to just drinking away their free time. The men thought very highly of Mr & Mrs Manisty.

A tug towing three canal barges down the Manchester Ship Canal, just above Eastham, c. 1896. Mount Manisty can be seen clearly in the background.

RIVER MERSEY

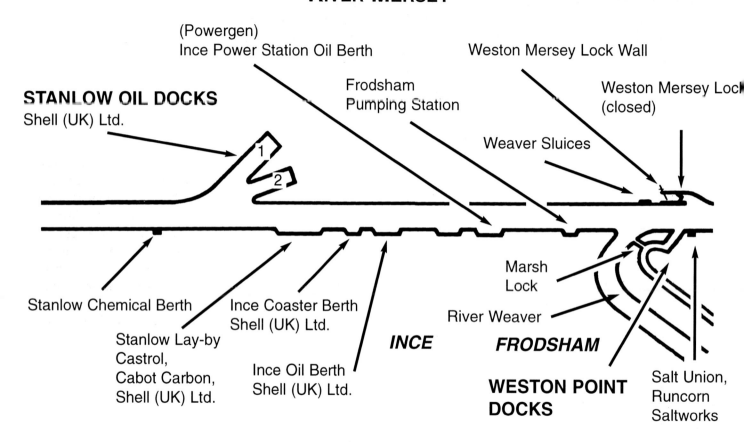

STANLOW OIL DOCKS
Shell (UK) Ltd.

(Powergen)
Ince Power Station Oil Berth

Frodsham
Pumping Station

Weston Mersey Lock Wall

Weston Mersey Lock
(closed)

Weaver Sluices

1

2

Stanlow Chemical Berth

Ince Coaster Berth
Shell (UK) Ltd.

Marsh
Lock

Stanlow Lay-by
Castrol,
Cabot Carbon,
Shell (UK) Ltd.

Ince Oil Berth
Shell (UK) Ltd.

INCE

River Weaver

FRODSHAM

**WESTON POINT
DOCKS**

Salt Union,
Runcorn
Saltworks

The divide between the Ship Canal and the River Mersey at this point is known as the Ellesmere Port Embankment. On the land side you see the STANLOW OIL REFINERY, the second in size and importance after London for the United Kingdom. In 1920 the amount of crude oil handled in the Canal rose dramatically as motor transport became more popular. The Ship Canal Company decided that it needed a special dock to handle this large influx of crude oil, and ever mindful of the safety in handling this very flammable import decided to build the new dock on the river side of the Canal. The mud flats and low ground at Stanlow was ideal, and in 1922 a dock was built there, with the pipes carrying the crude oil going underneath the Canal, and the safety standards imposed were the very highest possible. By the 1930's imports and exports of petroleum products had grown even more making it necessary to build another, larger dock. This new dock (No. 2, the larger) was opened on May 26th 1933 by the Minister of Transport Mr Oliver Stanley, when a B.P. tanker berthed there. That is the STANLOW OIL DOCKS on the river side of the Canal.

On the Manchester side of Stanlow Oil Docks, if you look closely, you will see the River Gowy which has crossed the Frodsham Plain, disappear under the Manchester Ship Canal and come out on the estuary side to join the River Mersey. This is a 'syphon' a piece of engineering where the sheer momentum of the river and the fact that the out-flow is lower than the in-flow, keep it working perpetually.

There are various oil berths as you pass the Ince Refinery and all are connected to unloading oil for onward movement to Stanlow.

Somewhere underneath the great Stanlow Oil Refinery are the remains of Stanlow Monastery a Benedictine Order under the Abbot of Chester, founded c. 1100. The first monks here found life extra hard, the land was too soft, cattle grazing was poor and boggy land made footpaths treacherous. Before the monastery was fully completed they had sought permission to move, ending up at Sawley near Clitheroe.

INCE: Once clear of the oil refinery, the area is called Ince. The word is Celtic meaning 'island', and it is probabley true as the Frodsham Marshes show many signs of being deep under water in the past. It is here that the River Mersey is at its widest roughly 3 miles across. Looking across the river you can make out Hale Lighthouse (now unused) on the Merseyside shore. It was by this lighthouse in about 1585, so legend says, that a young John Middleton went to sleep a normal sized man, and woke up 9ft 3ins tall. He was known as the 'Childe of Hale' and became so famous that even King James I came to visit him. He is buried in Hale Churchyard, and an Inn bearing his name makes Hale an interesting place to visit.

FRODSHAM: The farm of Frod, recorded in the Domesday Book as 'Frotesham' and is still pronounced that way by locals. 'Ham' is an old word to describe a settlement where everyone is related and under a father figure, so it would be more than just one fortified building, more like a small village. The hill at Frodsham shows many signs of early man. The plinth seen on top is Frodsham's War Memorial, but in the 1950's and 1960's the Merseyview Fairground was there, complete with helter-skelter right on the edge of the hill. The ballroom up there was very popular in the Swinging Sixties and saw all the top groups appearing there. Today it is an hotel called Forrest Hills, which commands magnificent views and it is well worth a trip up there.

HELSBY: The name is of Norse origin and denotes Viking influence. The difference between the two hills sharp and contrasting. Frodsham is lived on and well used, Helsby is, and always has been, dark and mysterious. When the local witch was put to death, the front of Helsby Hill fell away leaving her image up there in the rock. For many years her face was easy to make out, but now with time and the elements, you now only get an odd glimpse of the famous profile. Helsby Hill was the place where robbers were gibbeted and they hung for all to see from the Warrington/Chester main road. The caves behind Helsby have been found to contain the remains of wolves and bears.

Runcorn Docks showing the tidal dock looking from the Ship Canal.

There is another 'syphon' opposite Hale, which takes the Holpool Gutter (a small brook) under the Canal and into the River Mersey. The level of this brook is below the level of the Canal so it had to be syphoned underneath it. Look out for FRODSHAM PUMPING STATION: it is here where the dredgers unload the silt which is spread on the land behind the station. Some 900,000 cubic yards of silt and mud is annually removed from this section of the canal.

There are two in-flows into the canal, here. The RIVER WEAVER is nearest Eastham; the name of the river comes from Olde English 'wefer' a winding stream, and describes how the river weaves its way across the Cheshire Plain. Opposite the River Weaver you will see, set in the canal embankment, the unique River Weaver Sluices which allow the waters from the river to pass out into the River Mersey. It is important that this section (the longest between locks) stays at the same level. Ships tied up do not want the level of water altering, especially when discharging inflammable products. All rivers are not constant in the amount of water that flows down them, and the Weaver is no exception, these ten carefully controlled sluices (overflows) each 30ft wide, let out just the right amount of water to keep everything finely balanced.

It was here on the edge of the River Weaver that the settlement called 'Saltport' was built by the navvies working on the Ship Canal. This was not just living quarters for the workers but docking facilities for sailing ships taking out Cheshire salt to the world. There were also handling facilities for the barges bringing salt from the three Cheshire 'Wiches', Nantwich, Northwich, and Middlewich. The word 'wich' means 'special place' in Olde English. All three towns are on the River Weaver and since Roman times their precious commodity has been floated down the river and onwards to their eager customers. Coming down the river with the flow was easy, but it was hard work returning, especially after rain, and in the winter when the river ran fast. It was because of these difficulties that a canal was cut alongside the river and called the Weaver Navigation. Locks and weirs between the two kept the canal full of water but without the struggle against the flow. This navigation can be clearly made out next to the river and it runs alongside our Canal for some distance into Runcorn (Weston Point) Docks.

On the opposite bank of the Canal to the Weaver Sluices is the Castner Kelner Alkali Works, owned by ICI. This massive complex is lit day and night and has its own electricity supply. It was used in the filming of the early T.V. horror programmes 'Quatermass' and 'Quatermass and the Pit' made when television was still in black and white. Next to it is the RUNCORN SALT WORKS and in the embankment facing that is the WESTON MERSEY LOCK (now unused). This lock was built at Parliament's insistence so that barges and ships from the Weaver Basin could get out into a high-tide Mersey without going down the Eastham Locks.

There is a lot to see and a lot to tell you about in this section, so keep your wits about you over the next half hour. Coming up to Runcorn Docks you will see a church looking all on its own. The small 'Delamere Docks' are on the landward side so this puts the church on an island. Once the dock workers and Salt Union workers lived in rows of houses here, but all has been cleared away except for the church.

RUNCORN DOCKS can accommodate ships up to 3,000 tons and a draught of 17ft 6ins. There are three docks within the complex, Francis Dock, Alfred Dock and Fenton Dock handle ships up to 390ft long. Runcorn was once an important port on the Mersey and was for some time free of Liverpool tariffs and able to have its own Customs and Excise. These docks have always handled a very wide range of mixed goods and some surprising imports have been seen in the past. Guano (bat and bird droppings); cows horns and hide from South America; chemicals and ore from all over the world. Next to the dock once stood Bridgewater House, built by the Bridgewater Canal Company to control the connection from that canal down to the River Mersey, later the Ship Canal. In 1776 when the Bridgewater Canal reached Runcorn, a steep bank of 10 locks was constructed to bring the barges and packet boats down to the River Mersey where they could sail or be towed to Liverpool. Those locks and another set down from Doctor's Bridge to Runcorn Docks, cut through the banking here behind Bridgewater House. The Ship Canal Company moved out of this building in 1996 and within weeks the place suffered a large fire. Plans at the moment are to pull it down, though there is a strong voice to have it preserved. If you cannot see it, it has been pulled down. You are about to go under the RUNCORN - WIDNES RAILWAY BRIDGE, and the canal here is at its very narrowest, because the London North-Western Railway Company would not let the canal builders deepen the channel by the bridge support. When the bridge was constructed, starting in 1866, a clear head-way of 75ft had been stipulated by Parliament, that was on a tidal river, and today we have an 80ft clearance above us. Not many people know this, but the part of the bridge that we pass under is called the 'Ethelfleda' in honour of the daughter of King Offa of Mercia. It was she who established the first regular ferry across the river at this point. The railway bridge opened on May 21st 1868.

WIDNES: the name comes Wide Nes a wide nose shaped mound that was here until 1864 when it was used as banking for the railway bridge crossing the River Mersey. The area you see from the boat is called West Bank, but two centuries ago was known as Wood End (where the woods finish) and was a recommended bathing place for wealthy citizens from Manchester and Warrington. Sandy beaches, fresh salt air, sea breezes and medicinal mud were among the charms offered. Places do change don't they?

RUNCORN: the name comes from Olde English 'Rum' spacious, and 'Cofa' a cove. That is what was once here: A spacious cove. The word 'cofa' sometimes refers to chambers or even rooms, so there is even chance that the name could reflect a large cave in the area. Runcorn Hill has quarries which produced a lovely red sandstone. Liverpool Town Hall and the Anglican Cathedral both have parts built from Runcorn Stone.

The HIGH LEVEL ROAD BRIDGE here opened officially on Friday July 21st 1968 by HRH Princess Alexandra and took roughly five years to build including the approach roads and elevated sections. It too gives an 80ft clearance, though the top of the arch is 270ft above you. Now floodlit every night it is an impressive sight. Look quickly to the Runcorn side and you will notice a squarish base and a slip-

The Canal during construction on the bend past Runcorn Docks

way next to it. The slipway was the base for the Runcorn Ferry which was the only way to cross the river before May 1868 when a footpath opened along the railway bridge. The famous monologue ''Runcorn Ferry'' written by Marriott Edgar in the 1920's and immortalised by Stanley Holloway sums this up.

> *Now Runcorn lay over on one side of stream,*
> *And Widnes on t'other side stood;*
> *And as nobody wanted to go either place*
> *Well the trade wasn't any too good.*

The thought of the Ramsbottom family walking across the river, Albert under the water holding his mum's hand, and Ted the boatman holding out for

''Tuppence per person per trip'' always raises a laugh.

The Ferry was serious business and in the 1700's fiercely competed for. The Greenall family, of brewing fame, made some of its fortune by holding the Ferry Licence here for a few generations. In 1864 when the large Wesleyan Chapel opened in Widnes (now Queen's Hall) 300 people attended from Runcorn, and it took two hours to get them all across even with an extra boat.

The squarish raised base is all that is left of the famous WIDNES TRANSPORTER BRIDGE a marvellous feat of Edwardian engineering. It was like a giant Meccano structure, twin towers on either side with a 1,000ft span between that had a platform strung beneath it moving at 4 miles per hour from West Bank, Widnes, to Runcorn. It had electric motors on the gantry which powered, from its own source of electricity, the platform and its cargo on its three to four minute journey across the Mersey. The controller was in a cabin on top of the Pedestrian Shelter, and would stop above the Canal wall if any boats were passing. Opened May 29th 1905 it carried up to twelve motor cars and about a hundred people. It cost £135,000 to build, and was the largest transporter in the world, and one of only four built in this country. It closed on Saturday July 22nd 1961, the day after the road bridge opened, and cost £1,000 more to pull down than it cost to put up.

RUNCORN OLD QUAY is on the shore side and I hope you can see the canal gate repair shop here. The gates which hold back the water in the canal locks are made of greenheart wood, one of the hardest woods in the world. These gates which weigh around 250 tons and are 70ft high, have to be lifted on and off for maintenance by a special steam-powered crane. Some of the gates can usually be seen lying here. Opposite this facility is another of the disused locks allowing access into the river.

The river swings away here leaving land on both sides of the Canal, and on the land to the river side there is a large ICI Chemical Works (Wigg Works). To get to and from it you encounter the first of the five swing road bridges you will pass on your journey. THE OLD QUAY SWING BRIDGE gives an opening of 120ft when swung, and is 19ft above the canal when closed. You will be surprised how quickly these bridges swing aside and back into position.

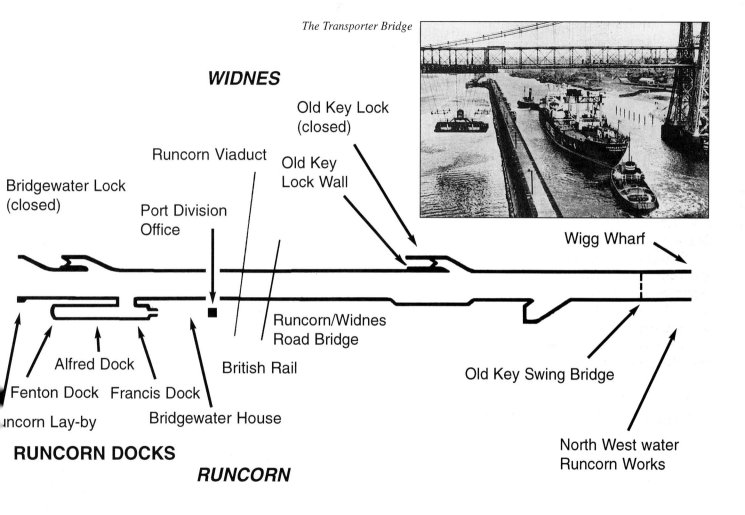

The Transporter Bridge

WIDNES

Old Key Lock
(closed)

Runcorn Viaduct

Old Key
Lock Wall

Bridgewater Lock
(closed)

Port Division
Office

Wigg Wharf

Runcorn/Widnes
Road Bridge

Alfred Dock

British Rail

Old Key Swing Bridge

Fenton Dock   Francis Dock

uncorn Lay-by

Bridgewater House

RUNCORN DOCKS

North West water
Runcorn Works

RUNCORN

The Manchester Ship Canal: under the Runcorn Bridge, a drawing from a century ago

Looking south at this point you should make out two structures against the sky-line.

Firstly HALTON CASTLE, built c. 1077 for Roger de Pictou when he took his title Baron of Runcorn. The castle passed into the Duke of Lancaster's hands when the Fifth Baron of Runcorn turned against the throne and then into a Royal Possession when Henry VII, Duke of Lancaster, ascended the throne. For hundreds of years this place was the court for both sides of the Mersey, and the castle was last used during the Civil War when it undertook a lengthy siege surrendering to the Roundheads on July 22nd 1643. The castle was then sacked on Cromwell's orders and has remained derelict ever since. The court house was used right up to this century, and is now the Halton Castle Hotel, technically owned by the Queen, and with a royal coat of arms over the door. Though I have not seen her behind the bar lately.

The round tower on the sky-line is the HALTON WATER TOWER, built by Liverpool Corporation. It is a pumping station for the water supply from Lake Vyrnwy in Wales to Liverpool. The massive pipe is taken underneath the canal and the River Mersey just here as we pass the Runcorn Water Works on the south side of the Canal.

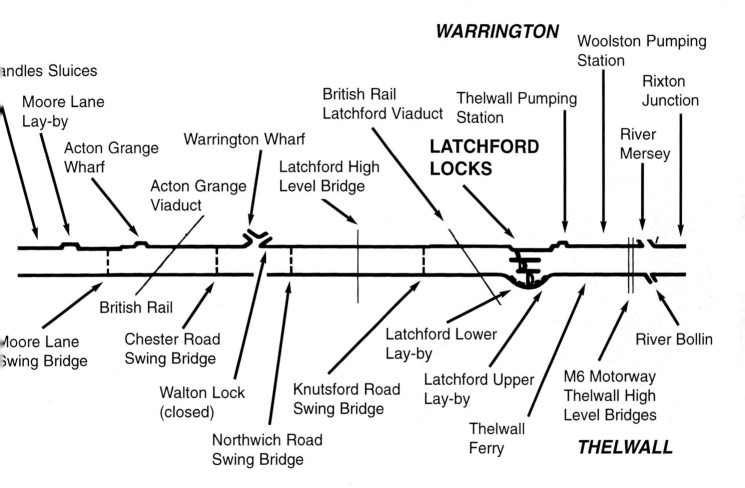

WARRINGTON

andles Sluices

Moore Lane Lay-by

Acton Grange Wharf

Acton Grange Viaduct

Warrington Wharf

British Rail Latchford Viaduct

Latchford High Level Bridge

Thelwall Pumping Station

LATCHFORD LOCKS

Woolston Pumping Station

Rixton Junction

River Mersey

British Rail

Moore Lane Swing Bridge

Chester Road Swing Bridge

Walton Lock (closed)

Knutsford Road Swing Bridge

Northwich Road Swing Bridge

Latchford Lower Lay-by

Latchford Upper Lay-by

Thelwall Ferry

M6 Motorway Thelwall High Level Bridges

River Bollin

THELWALL

You pass RANDLE SLUICES on the river (North side of the canal). Again put in to keep the water level constant. Look north and you will see the tall chimneys and cooling towers of Fiddler's Ferry Power Station. A coal-fired installation, which is thought to cause acid rain to fall in Denmark and Sweden. At least now they have identified the problem they are working hard to find a solution. FIDDLER'S FERRY was once an important fording point on the River Mersey, and now preserved at Norton Priory is a large statue of St. Christopher which once guarded the crossing.

NORTON PRIORY is just to the South of us. It was a monastery, one of those taken down on the orders of Henry VIII. The Moore family bought the land and built a mansion here where they lived and ruled for about four hundred years. The Priory is now a museum and exhibition centre, showing monastic life and the Priory ruins. A large rambling garden, and a wonderful walled garden with a pleasant refreshment area, makes the Priory well worth a visit.

MOORE LANE SWING BRIDGE moves aside leaving us 120ft of Canal to get by. This swing bridge has the lowest head room when closed, being only 10ft above the water. ACTON GRANGE WHARF once a loading point for the National Coalboard is to the North, and then we go under ACTON GRANGE RAILWAY VIADUCT. This bridge carries the main London-Glasgow railway line (the West Coast Line) and is electrified. It also carries the Manchester-Warrington-North Wales rail line, so there are four tracks above you. It has a 72ft clearance over the Canal and

opened in July 1893. It was the last bridge over the Canal to be passed fit before the Canal opened, and you are half-way in distance on your Canal trip as you pass under it.

CHESTER ROAD SWING BRIDGE pulls aside and as you pass you will notice traffic waiting either side to use the road. This is the A56 main road from Warrington to Chester and North Wales. The two swing bridges that we have already passed do not carry much road traffic, but this one does. The ferry is probably the only ship passing this way today, but can you imagine twenty to thirty ships per day, and twenty to thirty hold-ups. The Canal was not popular with motorists. Wave as you go by, won't you?

North of the Canal you will see a lock, WALTON LOCK (150ft by 28ft). Unused now, it once allowed vessels to re-join the original path of the River Mersey, and by a cut (diversion) they could take their cargoes right into the centre of Warrington, which is just over a mile North of you. WARRINGTON means the settlement or community by the weir in Olde English. Timber and leather hides were the main cargoes through this lock.

The NORTHWICH ROAD SWING BRIDGE is passed and again please wave at the waiting traffic using the A49 to Shrewsbury and Whitchurch. Just by the Manchester side of the swing bridge you may make out the remains of 'Twenty-Steps Lock' which went into what was the Runcorn to Latchford Canal, part of the Mersey and Irwell Navigation. Along with the Woolston Canal further up river, it enabled small barges to use the Navigation in summer droughts and winter floods. LATCHFORD HIGH LEVEL ROAD BRIDGE was built after the Canal opened and for the impatient motorist who could not wait for the swing bridge gates to re-open. A high level cantilever bridge, it was popular with locals and crosses at 72ft above the Canal. KNUTSFORD ROAD SWING BRIDGE is one of the heavier of the swing bridges weighing about 15 hundred tons. This carries the A50 which was the main road from Warrington (and all points North and West) down to London via Knutsford, Holmes Chapel and Stoke.

LATCHFORD RAILWAY VIADUCT is a good example of what had to be done to get the railway lines on to bridges with at least 70ft clearance. You can see to the North the immense amount of earthworks and embankment needed.

The railway bridge at Latchford that carried the Stockport to Warrington railway, high above the Ship Canal.

The original railway line had to stay in place while the bridge was being constructed, and the railway inspectors in February 1893 insisted that only goods trains could use the bridge for the first six months. They reasoned that if it collapsed with a goods train on it, only the driver and fireman would be at risk. The bridge and embankments were built by the Cheshire Line Committee, an amalgamation of railway companies who wanted running rights in the Lancashire/Cheshire area. They decided to build an alternative route between Liverpool and Manchester and went through Stockport by Altrincham, through Lymm into Warrington (Bank Quay Low Level). The line continued passed Fiddler's Ferry into South Widnes, Ditton Junction and on to Liverpool. It was quite successful for a time, but after British Rail came along it was used mostly for freight. A small service, Warrington, Lymm, Altrincham ran until the 1960's, and the line closed completely in 1989. There was a suggestion to re-open the line for trams a few years ago, but British Rail very quickly ripped up the track.

LATCHFORD LOCKS: There are two locks, the larger 600ft x 65ft, the smaller 350ft x 45ft. Having two locks was ideal when a ship was being towed or guided along the Canal. The tug would steer the ship into the larger lock and get into the smaller lock alongside without casting off the tow rope, saving time by being ready to guide the ship out and onwards. At Latchford your ferry will rise (or fall) by 12ft 6ins. The lock master's control room is on the North side of the lock, and from here they control not only

Latchford, but the next three locks as well. There is also a monitor and intruments keeping a careful eye, day and night, on the flow and amount of water in the upper reaches of the Canal. There is an ancient right of way across the Canal at this point, and today members of the public can cross via the canal gates and taking the path along the lock side. You will see members of the public crossing as you go through the locks. As you leave the locks on the North side you will see a factory built as the Richmond Gas Stove Company Works. Have you ever had a New World gas cooker? Well it was made here, the place where they made stove enamel gas cookers for the Gas Board after the war when everybody wanted a new fangled gas cooker.

THELWALL FERRY: Old Thelwall is a sleepy place, but it was once declared a city by Edward I. From here he sent his men to see if they could "repair and make good Manchester." On the south bank you will see a rowing boat, the last of the original ferries, and the boatman still turns out daily to take his regular passengers across. It costs 17p per crossing at the moment, and except for when a group turn up to cross "for the sheer joy of it", he has between 11 and 18 passengers a day, some just going across to exercise their dogs. Over the other side is the River Mersey and the Deposit Ground where the silt from the upper stretches of the Canal are spread. The Thelwall Pumping Station, which takes the silt and mud from the dredgers is opposite the ferry. THELWALL VIADUCT - a high level road bridge taking the M6 over the Mersey Valley. It crosses the Bridgewater Canal and the River Mersey as well as the Manchester Ship Canal. It was originally built as one bridge with three lanes each way, but 1996 saw the start of another bridge alongside so north and south bound traffic each have their own bridge today (opened 1997). You can clearly make out the two distinct bridges as you pass underneath.

You will notice some steel mesh on the banks of the Canal around here, these contain local rocks and bricks and were the brainchild of an Italian engineer, Sen. Gabbion. The spaces between the rocks soak up the wash from passing ships and saves the bank from erosion. Simple idea, but works very well. The RIVER BOLLIN comes in from the south, and try as they might historians cannot say where the name Bollin comes from. In the river entrance you will see three sunken concrete invasion barges, made ready to be towed down to the south coast in 1940. They were never sent for and have lain here ever since.

On the north side of the canal you see the RIVER MERSEY WEIR, where the River Mersey goes off on its own path towards Liverpool. It really is a marvellous feat of engineering, ingenuity and imagination, to canalise a river, and then let another river flow into the carefully managed volume and flow out 4 miles away. That is what happens here. The excess water poured in by the River Mersey further up-stream, now pours out over the weir and onward to keep the ferries moving between Liverpool and Birkenhead.

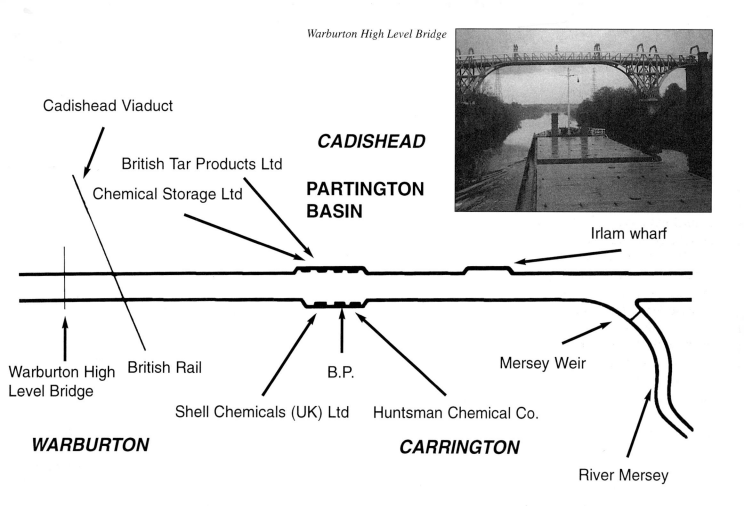

Warburton High Level Bridge

Cadishead Viaduct

CADISHEAD

British Tar Products Ltd

PARTINGTON BASIN

Chemical Storage Ltd

Irlam wharf

Warburton High Level Bridge

British Rail

B.P.

Mersey Weir

Shell Chemicals (UK) Ltd

Huntsman Chemical Co.

WARBURTON

CARRINGTON

River Mersey

Question; Where do you pay to cross a river that is no longer there.

Answer; Here, at the WARBURTON HIGH LEVEL ROAD BRIDGE.

To cross this high level road bridge and another small stone bridge, you are charged 10p per car, yet Parliament decreed that all crossings of the Manchester Ship Canal must be toll free. The high level bridge is free, paid for by the Ship Canal Company, to take travellers 74ft above the Canal made by a new cut in the canalization of the River Mersey. The little stone bridge was a toll bridge over the old River Mersey course, and it does not seem to matter that the river has been diverted, and that beneath the bridge is less than two foot of fresh air six foot wide. Much to the annoyance of the Canal Company, the de Trafford family continued to collect the toll after the Ship Canal opened and indeed the executors of the de Trafford family still collect the toll today. Do not forget that you are travelling on a river made into a canal, and bits of the old river course can be seen on the South side next to the Warburton Bridge.

CADISHEAD VIADUCT: A high level railway bridge, now disused, and in a very poor state of repair. It was built to carry the Cheshire railway lines 73ft 9ins above the Canal, as the company built a railway line from Stockport to Wigan. It really will not last much longer, and is expected to be taken down very soon.

When the Canal first opened, 90% of the traffic was steamers, and 10% sail. Ships needed re-coaling, and it was here at PARTINGTON COALING STAGE that they filled their bunkers with Lancashire coal to power them across the oceans. To begin with coal came from the Worsley coalmines of the Bridgewater Canal Company, but when oil and diesel superseded coal, this place became the 'garage' for the Canal. Still here today is the chemical facilities, and Shell and BP unloading points.

IRLAM AND CADISHEAD are to the North of you, and PARTINGTON to the South. The Irlam wharf on the North was once a very busy spot. Irlam Steel Works was next to the Canal and was one of the biggest steel works in England. Built by the Lancashire Steel Company, it was a hive of industry and 30 years ago the night sky would be lit up with fires and sparks.

The River Mersey itself comes in from the south, after making its way from Stockport. The River Mersey (the word Mersey means boundary) does not rise in the Pennines or trickle poetically down hillsides, it begins where the Rivers Goyt and Tame join, along side the the M60 at Stockport, that is when the name Mersey first appears.

The Partington Oil Basin today, still very much in use.

The now disused Cadishead Viaduct, one of the massive railway bridges over the Canal.

The lovely peaceful village of Barton-upon-Irwell as it was before the Ship Canal was built. Note the strong stone bridges that were there before it became necessary to construct swinging bridges to allow the large sea-going vessels to pass.

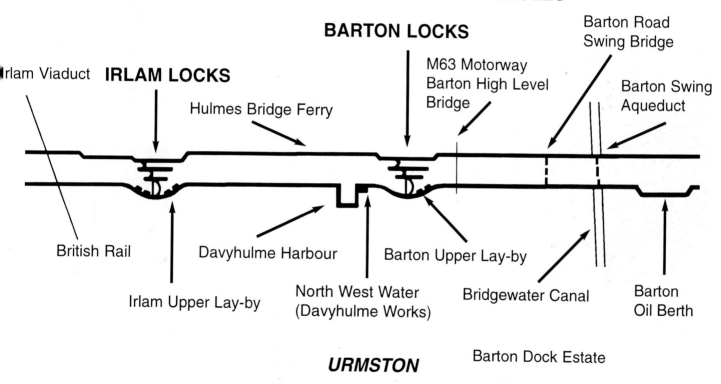

ECCLES

BARTON LOCKS

Irlam Viaduct IRLAM LOCKS

M63 Motorway
Barton High Level
Bridge

Barton Road
Swing Bridge

Barton Swing
Aqueduct

Hulmes Bridge Ferry

British Rail

Davyhulme Harbour

Barton Upper Lay-by

Irlam Upper Lay-by

North West Water
(Davyhulme Works)

Bridgewater Canal

Barton
Oil Berth

URMSTON

Barton Dock Estate

IRLAM VIADUCT: A high level railway bridge which carries the Manchester Liverpool line. This is the original railway, opened in 1830, and later ran from Liverpool Central to Manchester Central. Still in use today, it gives a clearance of 73ft 7ins above the Canal. Though we have left the River Mersey's influence, we are still in a canalized river. This section is the River Irwell (Irrc is Olde English for winding and Wella is spring). Irlam is the family settlement by the Irwell - Irewelhan later Irlam.

IRLAM LOCKS: Two locks, the same size as Latchford and Barton, 600ft x 65ft and the smaller 350ft x 45ft . Here we have the largest step of the internal locks on the Canal, and the ferry rises (or falls) 16ft. Thousands of gallons of water are pumped into the lock to raise us to the next level. There is a right-of-way over these locks today, granted after the Irlam Ferry ceased. Locals would use it as a short cut perhaps to the CWS Soap Works that are on the north side of the locks. On the Manchester side near the lock, you can clearly make out where the ferry was. At one time it was a vehicular ferry and could take one car or van across the Canal. This was replaced by a pull across ferry called the "Transverse." The road running on the North side of the Canal is only a few years old, and is the Irlam and Cadishead by-pass.

Another abandoned ferry is the Hulme's Bridge Ferry. Wherever there was a bridge or ford, the Canal Company were compelled to build a bridge or provide a ferry. They talk of Australia's Sydney Harbour and its sweeping bay,

Barton Locks from the air taken 7th November 1952. The picture shows the 'Caledonia' on the left outward bound for the open sea, and another vessel waiting to head into Salford Docks.

and they sing of San Fransico's Harbour well here is DAVY-HULME HARBOUR! That is the official title of the four berth installation on the South of the Canal. Owned by Manchester Corporation Water Works, it is connected directly to their Davyhulme Sewage Works. At one time, quite a lot of excess effluent was taken down the Canal and dumped over the bar in Liverpool Bay, but thanks to better sewage treatments, this traffic has almost stopped.

BARTON LOCKS: Two locks, one large, one small. Same size as the last two, 600ft x 54ft and 350ft x 45ft. At this lock the rise, or fall is 15ft. This is the most out of the way of all of the locks and is over a mile from the nearest road.

BARTON HIGH LEVEL ROAD BRIDGE: Built to take the M63 South from its junction with the M62 at Eccles. The road is now re-numbered as the M60 - Manchester Orbital Motorway. It is 81ft 6ins clearance above the Canal, and is the highest of the bridges on our journey. Opened in 1960 it took three years to complete and they seem to have been working on it ever since.

Look south and you can see the domes of the TRAFFORD SHOPPING CENTRE, one of the largest shopping centres in Britain, and opened in September 1998. Built by Peel Holdings, who also own and run the Manchester Ship Canal. Make sure you are looking South as you approach (or leave) BARTON ROAD SWING BRIDGE. There in the trees you will see, set among an overgrown graveyard, a 200-ton piece of Cornish Granite 18ft x 21ft with the word Stevens on it. This marks the last resting place of MARSHALL STEVENS. See page 8. He was General Manager of the Ship Canal all through the years of building and during its first years after opening. Many historians are convinced, that but for him, the Canal would not have been built. He also made TRAFFORD PARK a success, and wanted to be buried where he could see the ships go past and hear the sounds from Trafford Park. He was also MP for Eccles, so what a fitting resting place for this man. Next to the Barton Road Swing Bridge you will see the tower of BARTON MONASTERY built as All Saints R.C. Church in 1864 by E. W. Pugin for the de Trafford family. The church was declared redundant and taken over in 1962 by the monks of the Friars Minor Conventual of the Benedictine Order. It was restored to its former glories between 1985 and 1991. The order trains brothers for missionary work here, and sends out a magazine "The Crusader" to the whole of the world.

BARTON ROAD SWING BRIDGE: 195ft long there is not as wide an opening here, only 90ft as apposed to 120ft at the other swing bridges. The bridge turns on 64 steel rollers. We then pass the unique swing bridge, the BARTON AQUEDUCT (bridge carrying water [aqua, latin] over water). When the river was just a Navigation this was the village of Barton-upon-Irwell and fitted snugly on either side of the river. The road bridge here was wide enough to take a cart and people walking and the Duke's Canal crossed on a fine stone bridge lined with clay. The Bridgewater

Canal ran from Worsley, and from 1766 overcame its main obstacle, the River Irwell by bridging it with an aqueduct. Coal was brought down in large canvas bags which were lowered from the canal level down to boats on the Irwell below, then horse-drawn into Manchester. The price of coal dropped from 7d to 4d a bag when this system was introduced and coal became more plentiful and cheaper for the poor of the town. By 1775 the facilities at the Manchester end of the Bridgewater Canal had been completed and there was no need for the interchange as coal just carried on to Castlefield where coal yards were opened and coal prices fell again.

BARTON SWING AQUADUCT: Built between 1892 and first filled with water on June 14th 1893. The first boat to pass over it was the 'Ann' on August 21st of that year. The aqueduct is 235ft long, 23ft 9ins wide and 33ft high. The tank which contains the water is 18ft wide and 7ft deep (six foot of water). When it swings it weights 1450-tons, of which 800-ton is water. Designed by E. Leader Williams of the Ship Canal Company, it has remained virtually unchanged, except that the walk-way for horses who pulled the barges has been taken down, since it was built. When first opened, both bridges were swung by hydraulic water power, but today, both have electric pumps to push them round.

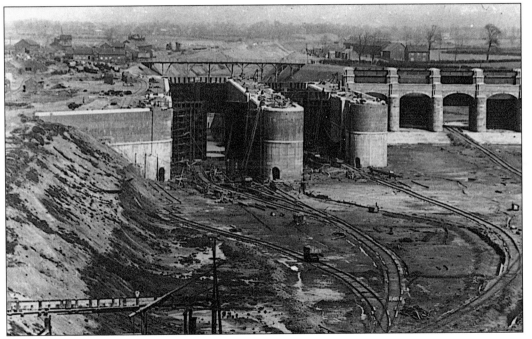

Locks and Sluices at Irlam under construction

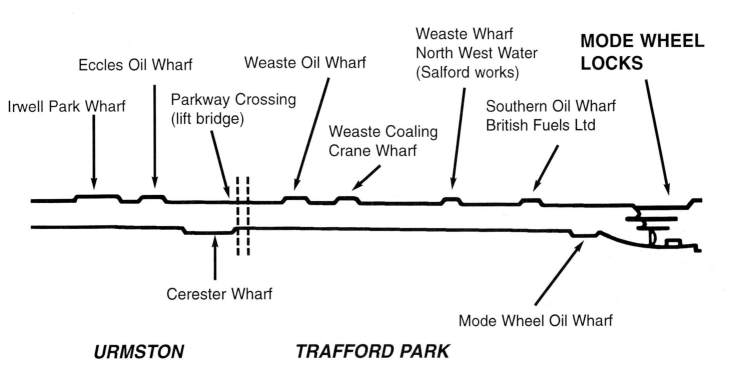

SALFORD

Weaste Wharf
North West Water
(Salford works)

**MODE WHEEL
LOCKS**

Eccles Oil Wharf

Weaste Oil Wharf

Southern Oil Wharf
British Fuels Ltd

Irwell Park Wharf

Parkway Crossing
(lift bridge)

Weaste Coaling
Crane Wharf

Cerester Wharf

Mode Wheel Oil Wharf

URMSTON

TRAFFORD PARK

49

The area on the North side of the canal, now a housing estate, was from the Canal first opening until 1970 a wood seasoning area. Timber, especially hardwood would be imported from Eastern Europe and allowed to season in small piles here. One story told to me by a former dock policeman about this bit of the canal IRWELL PARK WHARF concerns a German U-Boat captured in Liverpool Bay and moored here waiting to be examined. The submarine was brought up the canal in the morning and created a stir amongst local youngsters. In the afternoon a party of dockers stripped the vessel of all food supplies and piled them on the quayside. They then removed all the ammunition and torpedoes which were taken away by the army. As dusk gathered so did the youngsters determined to catch a glimpse of a real German U-Boat. Two or three boys were reported climbing the wall near the swing bridge with tins in their hands, and a scallywag was caught with packets of dried something up his jersey sneaking through the Timber Wharf Gates. Whatever happened that night, as the sun came up, every item of food had vanished. As the labels and instructions were in German, locals would not know whether it was dried soup or dried semolina, tinned peaches or tinned pears, but twelve months worth of supplies all disappeared during the night.

ECCLES OIL WHARF: now used to store scrap metal which the 'Arklow' boats take back down the Canal after they have brought grain up to CERESTAR WHARF opposite. One tanker can do the work of more than 20 heavy lorries, and this run on the Canal helps keep traffic down. The scrap goes to Spain and other European ports, and the grain comes mostly from Canada. Cerestar Wharf is on the southern bank next to the new bridge, and you may see one of the green (Irish based) boats such as the 'Arklow Trader' here unloading grain straight into the silos on the plant.

CENTENARY BRIDGE: The first lifting bridge over the Ship Canal. Opened in November of the Centenary of the Ship Canal 1894 - 1994 by Her Majesty Queen Elizabeth II. It takes less than a minute for the road-way to be raised

The Swinging Aquaduct at Barton

73ft 6ins above the water level, and when the road is down it has a clearance of 22ft 10ins so that barges and pleasure craft can pass under it without it being raised. You can see a Flour Mill being built on the North bank, and next to it an over-head pipe line constructed by Proctor & Gamble the toiletry makers. Do not worry you will not hit it, as as 88ft 6 ins it is higher than the Barton High Level Road Bridge.

TRAFFORD PARK: Is the industrial area to the South of the Canal here, and it stretches roughly for four miles along this bank. Once it was an ancestral home, like Chatsworth or Tatton Hall. It was the seat of the (de) Trafford family, and though they had owned the land since before Norman times, they moved here and made it their main residence after their other house in Old Trafford was disturbed by the building of the Bridgewater Canal in 1765. The family enlarged the hall and settled here for 125 years of peaceful and powerful living until the Ship Canal plans emerged in 1890. The de Traffords fought the plans and opposed the Ship Canal, but when the Canal Bill was passed, and old Sir Humphrey had died, the young heir decided to move away and sell the estate. Trafford Park ended up in the hands of an estate company who started its development as an industrial complex. The General Manager of that company, was the man who had guided the Ship Canal to success, MARSHALL STEVENS. He found that Manchester firms did not want to move into the Park, and went further afield to bring customers to his factories. He brought in Westinghouse and Fords from America, he attracted Kilverts and Brookbond

and again he made a success. While the Industrial Park was spreading slowly across the green acres, he allowed a variety of other money making ventures. Barnum & Bailey held a Three-Ring-Circus here for six months, a golf course was developed using the old Hall as an hotel. He built a whole estate for the workers, complete with school, church and pub. Boating took place on the Park lake and boat building was prominent. Manchester's very first air strip was in Trafford Park. In both the first and second world wars, Trafford Park, Britain's very first industrial park, played an important and key role.

The Park's fortunes have waxed and waned over the century since it was started, and now it is definitely on the up and up. The units may be smaller, the industry lighter, and it will never get back to the figure of 70,000 who worked here during and after W.W. 2. There are more and more firms finding that Trafford Park is the place where they feel they can grow and prosper. The plans to put Manchester's Metrolink through the Park and on to the Trafford Shopping Centre, can only bring more firms, jobs and prosperity.

MODE WHEEL LOCKS: There has been a lock or weir just here for more than 250 years. The original name was Maud's Wheel and there was a water-driven wheel which powered the mill at this point. Two locks, the larger 600ft x 65ft and the other 350ft x 45ft. Here our ferry will rise or fall 13ft and we will enter the complex that was SALFORD DOCKS.

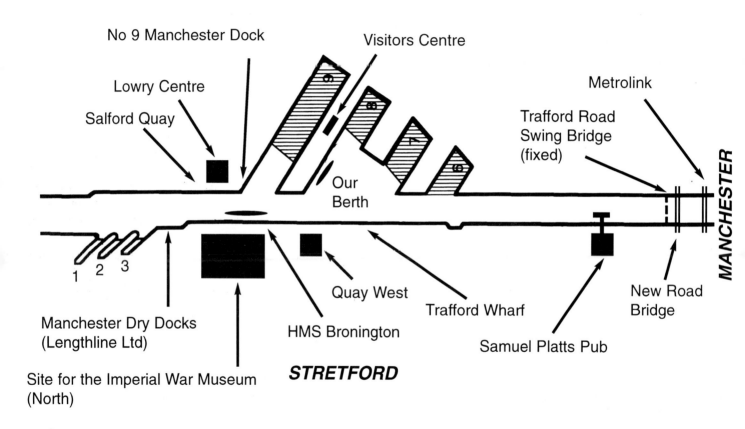

No 9 Manchester Dock

Visitors Centre

Metrolink

Lowry Centre

Trafford Road
Swing Bridge
(fixed)

Salford Quay

Our
Berth

MANCHESTER

1 2 3

Quay West

New Road
Bridge

Manchester Dry Docks
(Lengthline Ltd)

HMS Bronington

Trafford Wharf

Samuel Platts Pub

Site for the Imperial War Museum
(North)

STRETFORD

MANCHESTER DRY DOCKS: On the southern side of Mode Wheel Locks. There are three dry docks here, and although independent now, they were opened by the Manchester Ship Canal Company in 1905. The dry docks are (1) 535ft x 65ft, (2) 500ft x 65ft and (3) 450ft x 65ft, and they can handle Isle of Man boats, millionaires yachts and tugs as well as our own Mersey ferries. Always worth a close look at what is in the docks, it is a busy place.

On the same side you will find moored HMS 'Bronington' a de-commissioned mine sweeper that was once commanded by Prince Charles. The ship is open to the public, and as well as seeing one of the Navy's hardest working vessels you can view the Royal Cabin complete with Royal Hotline, see pictures of the Prince at sea, and visit the bridge and crews quarters - very interesting. The golden glass building next to it is Quay West an example of modern architecture at its best. Amongst the tenants of this building are Peel Holdings who control and run the Manchester Ship Canal and Bridgewater. Light A.M. also broadcast from this building. Salford Quays seems to be an attraction to Radio Stations. Jazz F.M. broadcasts from the other side of the Trafford Road Swing Bridge (now fixed) ahead, and Century Radio from the tall building to the North.

The Quayside next to the Bronington is where the IMPERIAL WAR MUSEUM OF THE NORTH is to be built. Work on the site is due to start at first light on Jan 1st 2000, to make it the first Millennium Project for the area.

The building activity taking place opposite Quay West is the L.S. LOWRY CENTRE, a millennium project created to show off the works of LAURENCE STEVEN LOWRY that are in the possession of Salford Corporation, as well as a theatre and arts centre combined. It is due to open at Easter in the year 2000 and is on schedule. A bridge is under construction between the centre and the area where 'Bronington' is moored.

As the ferry leaves or enters its berth at the end of what was No. 9 Dock, you can see a building in the canal near the Trafford Road Bridge, it has a walk-way connecting it to the "Samuel Platt" hotel and pub. It is in fact a restaurant and bar built on what was the pivot for a swinging railway bridge that was here. The concrete base has provided a perfect site for this hexagonal building and the nautical theme is carried on inside. "Samuel Platt" was the name of the brewer whose yacht the 'Norseman' carried Ship Canal directors up from Latchford on the opening day January 1st 1894. There is a wonderful collection of photographs and memorabilia in the pub, mixing history with a drink. The railway bridge has been moved, and now spans the large No. 9 Dock as a walk-way.

SALFORD DOCKS: The real title THE DOCKS OF THE MANCHESTER SHIP CANAL COMPANY. They were constructed in 1893-4 as loading and unloading facilities for the Ship Canal Company, and were completely run and operated by the Canal Company who had their own police force and fire brigade. Though the Company referred to them as Manchester Docks, 70% are actually in Salford, and as the dock gates were in Salford, and most of the work-force came from there, the men referred to them as Salford Docks. Just half of No. 1 Dock was actually inside the boundaries of Manchester. No. 2 and 3 Docks, Trafford Wharf, and the dry docks were in Stretford (now Trafford MBC). The docks at one time employed about 1,500 men. The variety of goods that came in and out of here was very extensive, and in early days there was a large trade of live cattle from Canada which was slaughtered in an abattoir near the site of the Dry Docks. The first Ford cars came in here in packing cases, and Henry Rolls (Rolls Royce) made cars and cranes next to Trafford Wharf. Generators for the luxury liners of the 1920's and 30's left here on ships for the builder's yards. The Metropolitan Carriage Company made railway carriages in Trafford Park for many foreign railways, and they were shipped from here to India, Australia and South America. The first boxes of Corn Flakes from Kelloggs in America came into here, and when they were successful, Kelloggs built their first U.K. plant nearby in Trafford Park. During the war there was so much European rail traffic being built here, that special lines were laid to the wide European gauge so that the engines, transformers etc., could be moved to the docks easier. The rail-mounted generators that did so much to bring victory on the Russian Front were all made in Trafford Park and shipped out from here.

The Salford dock workers always said that they could turn round a ship two days quicker than any other port, including Liverpool, thus making up the one-and-a-half days transversing the Ship Canal.

An aerial view of Salford Docks & Trafford park.

There is a very lively Heritage Centre on Salford Docks. It is situated in a large pre-fabricated building on No. 8 Dock next to the Quay House Hotel and Restaurant. The displays there are changed regularly and there is always a good representation of life and work on Salford Docks. It is very well worth visiting.

Our Mersey ferry is usually berthed in what was the large No.8. Dock (Central Bay). Originally there were three docks in this part, 6, 7 and 8. The largest, No.9 Dock, was added in 1913 but today access to it is cut off, and it is known as Huron & Erie Basin. Across No. 8 is a Bailey bridge and a thriving water sports centre. Inside the cut off dock, oxygen is pumped into the water and fish have been introduced into the docks. The extra cuts and water-ways here have been named to commemorate ties with Canada and USA. Many of the new roads built on ex-docks land also reflect the trans-Atlantic trade in their names.

Where No.9 Dock stands, was, for a time, the site of Manchester Race Course, and when the dock was built the grandstands were left up for guests to watch the King and Queen perform the opening ceremony. The races had gone back to their older site at Castle Irwell, Salford. Docks No. 1, 2, 3 & 4 are the other side of the Trafford Road Bridge, and only accessible to narrow boats and low pleasure craft. The official end of the Manchester Ship Canal is also there, another mile up stream from where we berth. Our water-way then becomes the River Irwell and goes on to divide Manchester and Salford. There was never a No.5 Dock, it was marked out but never cut.

Manchester Docks at war. A grain ship having run the gauntlet of the North Sea convoys in her battleship grey, unloads the precious cargo onto barges in the autumn of 1943.

An aerial view of Mode Wheel Locks in the 1930's. To the right is Manchester Dry Docks, which are still working today.

One of the later vessels belonging to the Company the 'Manchester Renown', built in 1964 ready for the container traffic, but it only worked for about 7 years before being sold off.

A Royal Navy vessel seen here at Latchford heading for Manchester Docks in 1932.

One of Her Majesty's Submarines leaving Manchester after an official visit in 1934.

October 1963 saw another Royal Navy visit to Salford Docks. Here we see a submarine arriving to join a sister sub. in delighting the public, on an open day.

Always plenty to see from the Mersey ferries as they sail the Manchester Ship Canal.

The 'Overchurch' enters a lock ready to descend to the next section.

Mersey Ferries

RIVER CRUISES - A 50 minute cruise, complete with spectacular views of Liverpool's waterfront, plus a lively and informative commentary. Leaves Pier Head, Liverpool every hour between 10 a.m -3 p.m. (6 p.m. at weekends).

SEACOMBE AQUARIUM - Located inside the Seacombe terminal, the aquarium provides a fascinating insight into the secret world that thrives beneath the river. Play 'hide and seek' with the sharks and rays, see the octopus's garden and get splashed by the mighty wave machine.

PIRATE'S PARADISE SOFT PLAY AREA - Also located inside the Seacombe terminal. Junior smugglers and pirates are able to raid a pirate ship and fight off giant crabs in the ball pool in search for buried treasure.

SOUVENIRS AND REFRESHMENTS - Gift shops at Pier Head, Seacombe and Woodside sell a wide range of souvenirs with decidedly nautical theme, from captains' hats to hand-painted model ferries. Refreshments are available at each of the terminals. Why not break your journey at Woodside and sample the delights of the Edwardian Restaurant?

SPECIAL CRUISES - During the summer Mersey Ferries operates a number of longer themed cruises for all the family.

CHILDREN'S EVENTS - Special cruises for children operate at Easter, school summer holidays, Hallowe'en and Christmas - or why not treat them to a birthday party on board?

CHARTER HIRE - Mersey Ferries are also available for Charter Hire to celebrate your own special event or company promotion. Full catering services available.

For further details on any of the above services please call...

Mersey Ferries on 0151 630 1030

The end of what we hope has been a perfect day. " I always said I would take you on a cruise."

THERE IS ALWAYS SOMETHING HAPPENING WITH MERSEY FERRIES.

PICK UP A LEAFLET NOW. RING 0151 630 1030 FOR DETAILS